D1070062

FROGS

Please visit our web site at: www.garethstevens.com
For a free color catalog describing Gareth Stevens Publishing's
list of high-quality books and multimedia programs, call
1-800-542-2595 (USA) or 1-800-387-3178 (Canada).
Gareth Stevens Publishing's fax: (414) 332-3567.

Library of Congress Cataloging-in-Publication Data

All about frogs.
    Frogs.
        p. cm. — (All about wild animals)
    Previously published in Great Britain as: All about frogs. 2002.
    ISBN 0-8368-4184-0 (lib. bdg.)
    1. Frogs—Juvenile literature.   I. Title.   II. Series.
    QL668.E2A45   2004
    597.8′9—dc22
                                                    2004040812

This edition first published in 2005 by
Gareth Stevens Publishing
A World Almanac Education Group Company
330 West Olive Street, Suite 100
Milwaukee, Wisconsin 53212 USA

This U.S. edition copyright © 2005 by Gareth Stevens, Inc. Original edition
copyright © 2002 by DeAgostini UK Limited. First published in 2002 as
My Animal Kingdom: All About Frogs by DeAgostini UK Ltd., Griffin House,
161 Hammersmith Road, London W6 8SD, England. Additional end matter
copyright © 2005 by Gareth Stevens, Inc.

Editorial and design: Tucker Slingsby Ltd., London
Gareth Stevens series editor: Catherine Gardner
Gareth Stevens art direction: Tammy West

Picture Credits
Animals Animals / Oxford Scientific Films — Gerlach: 19.
NHPA — Stephen Dalton: 7, 13, 21, 24–25, 25, 29; Laurie Campbell: 12;
    Martin Wendler: 13; William Paton: 20; Manfred Danegger: 23; Mirko
    Stelzner: 26–27; G. I. Bernard: 28; Daniel Heuclin: 29.
Oxford Scientific Films — Manfred Prefferle: front cover, title page, 15, 27;
    Paul Franklin: 6–7, 15; Mark Hamblin: 8, 23; Paulo de Oliveira: 9; Arthur
    Butler: 10; Jim Frazier: 11; G. I. Bernard: 14; Michael Fogden: 16, 19;
    Konrad Wothe: 18; John Cooke: 21; Owen Newman: 22; Mike Linley: 26.

Printed in the United States of America

1 2 3 4 5 6 7 8 9 08 07 06 05 04

FROGS

Gareth Stevens Publishing
A WORLD ALMANAC EDUCATION GROUP COMPANY

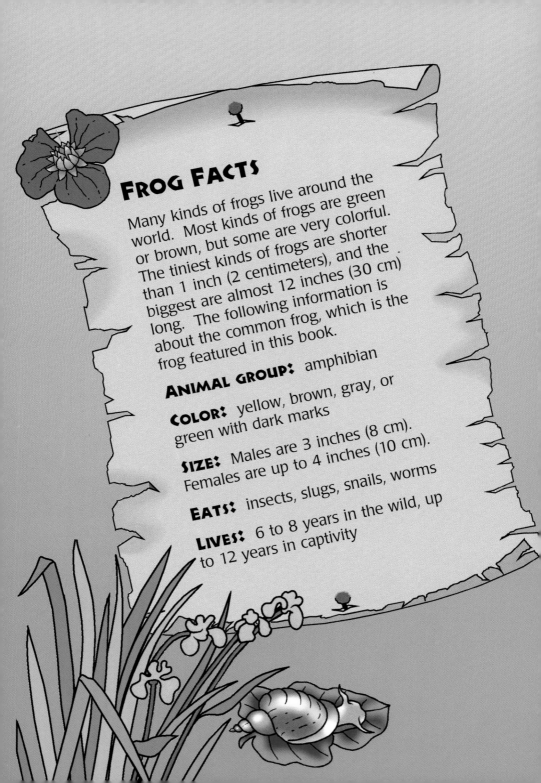

Frog Facts

Many kinds of frogs live around the world. Most kinds of frogs are green or brown, but some are very colorful. The tiniest kinds of frogs are shorter than 1 inch (2 centimeters), and the biggest are almost 12 inches (30 cm) long. The following information is about the common frog, which is the frog featured in this book.

Animal Group: amphibian

Color: yellow, brown, gray, or green with dark marks

Size: Males are 3 inches (8 cm). Females are up to 4 inches (10 cm).

Eats: insects, slugs, snails, worms

Lives: 6 to 8 years in the wild, up to 12 years in captivity

CONTENTS

Words that appear in the glossary
are printed in **boldface** type the
first time they occur in the text.

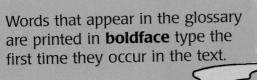

A Closer Look

Frogs are amphibians. Amphibians are animals that are as good at jumping across land as they are at swimming through water. There are many different kinds of frogs. Although their colors and sizes are different, their body shapes are similar. Most frogs have flat heads, wide mouths, and big eyes. Most frogs' bodies and front legs are small, but their back legs are strong. Many frogs can leap about twenty times their own body length!

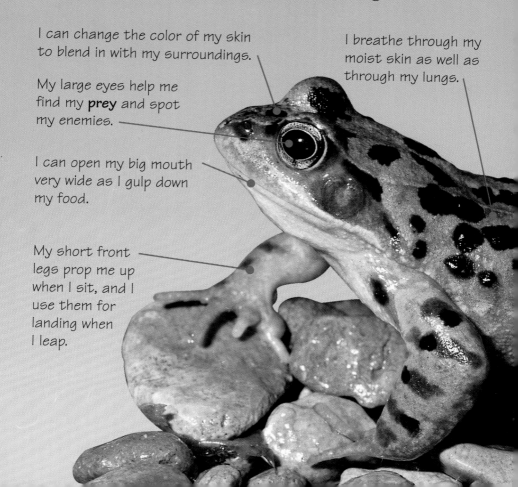

I can change the color of my skin to blend in with my surroundings.

My large eyes help me find my **prey** and spot my enemies.

I can open my big mouth very wide as I gulp down my food.

My short front legs prop me up when I sit, and I use them for landing when I leap.

I breathe through my moist skin as well as through my lungs.

- The word *amphibian* means "double life." A frog begins its life in the water and ends its life on land. Many kinds of frogs only return to ponds in order to **breed** and produce their own baby frogs.

- One reason frogs can live on both land and water is that they breathe through their lungs and their thin, moist skin.

- Frogs shed their skin every few weeks. Some kinds of frogs eat the skin that they shed.

- Some kinds of frogs can adjust their skin color to match the colors in their surroundings.

- Many frogs have poison in their skin that helps protect them from their enemies.

My strong back legs help me swim in the water and jump over the land.

The webbed toes on my back feet help me speed through water.

A frog has big eyes that bulge out, so it can see in just about any direction. A frog also has big ears, but they are hard to see. Frogs do not have ear flaps like humans do. A frog's ears are covered with flat discs of skin. Most frogs have good senses of touch and taste. They often spit out bad-tasting food! The kinds of frogs that live underground or hunt at night have a good sense of smell.

Flat discs, called tympanums, cover my ears. I can hear the softest sounds.

My bulging eyes help me look all around. I have two outer eyelids to protect each eye and a third, inner, eyelid.

My nostrils are on top of my nose.

My wide mouth is just right for catching prey. I can grab a meal with a quick flick of my long, sticky tongue.

A TRICKY TONGUE

Most frogs have very long tongues that are both quick and sticky. When a frog hunts food, it sits still until its prey is within its reach. Snap! The frog quickly flicks its tricky tongue. It catches its prey on the sticky tip of its tongue and pulls its meal into its wide mouth.

DID YOU KNOW?

A frog's big eyes come in handy for more than finding food. As a frog swallows its prey, it closes its eyes and pulls its eyeballs into its head. The eyeballs help push down on the frog's food, forcing its dinner to go down its throat.

HOME, SWEET HOME

Frogs live in almost every part of the world. They make their homes in grasslands, swamps, forests, deserts, and caves and also on mountains. Most frogs need to keep their skin wet, so they live near water or in damp places.

Different **species** of frogs live in different parts of the world and are known by many different names. The common frog is also called a European frog, grass frog, or brown frog. It lives in Europe and Asia.

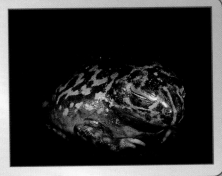

A frog is cold-blooded, which means that its body cannot make its own heat. To cool off or warm up, a frog must move to a colder or warmer place. During cold seasons, frogs **hibernate** until warm weather returns. Some lie in the mud at the bottom of a river or pond. Others **burrow** into the ground.

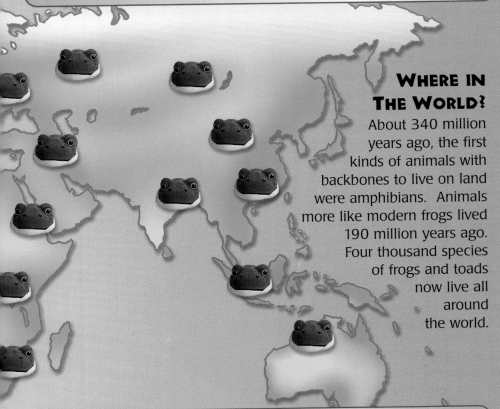

WHERE IN THE WORLD?

About 340 million years ago, the first kinds of animals with backbones to live on land were amphibians. Animals more like modern frogs lived 190 million years ago. Four thousand species of frogs and toads now live all around the world.

WATER-HOLDING FROG

Some types of frogs, such as the Australian water-holding frog, live in dry parts of the world. To keep its body moist when it cannot find water, this frog burrows into the damp dirt. Water it stores in the outer layers of its skin makes a kind of underground pool for the frog.

NEIGHBORS

Common frogs can live almost anywhere as long as there is water nearby. Hundreds of animals live alongside frogs. On land, neighbors of the common frog are insects, small **mammals**, and birds. They depend on grasses, other soft plants, and seeds for food. Worms and slugs crawl in the grass and dirt. In the water, the common frog meets fish, waterbirds, and lots of tiny creatures.

WATERY HOME

Frogs share their watery home with many other animals. Fish, such as **roaches**, search for food in the muddy bottom. Water beetles and other insects flit across the surface of the water. Newts, which are amphibians that look like lizards, hunt for small snails that crawl along the edges of rivers and ponds. Waterbirds dive for plants and animals that live in the water.

TAILS UP

Many different waterbirds live near ponds and rivers. Ducks float on the surface. They dunk their heads into shallow water to scoop up small water plants, insects, and even **tadpoles** and young frogs.

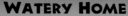

HOP ALONG!

Grasshoppers make
their homes in spots
where they can find
a lot of juicy leaves
and grass to nibble.
Grasshoppers blend
in with the colors of
the grass and plants
where they sit. Like
frogs, these amazing
jumpers use their
long, strong back
legs to leap from
place to place.
They are crunchy
prey for hungry frogs!

DARTING DRAGONFLIES

The brilliant blue emperor dragonfly
lives near ponds and rivers. It feeds
on insects that it plucks out of the air
with its legs and shovels into its huge
jaws. Dragonflies fly fast, and frogs
must be quick to catch them!

THE FAMILY

Most of the time, frogs live alone, but they get together in big groups to breed. For common frogs, breeding begins in spring, when they often return to the pond where they were born. The males usually arrive first. Then they start croaking loudly to attract the females and to warn off any **rival** males. After breeding, males and females go their separate ways. They do not stay together to protect their eggs or to raise their young tadpoles.

Most female frogs lay eggs, called spawn, in water. The eggs hatch into tiny tadpoles that do not look anything like their mothers. Tadpoles have no legs, so they cannot jump. They use their wiggly tails to swim in the water and breathe through **gills** the way that fish do. As young tadpoles grow, they go through a **metamorphosis**. They develop legs for hopping and lungs for breathing. Soon, baby frogs grow up to look just like their parents.

DID YOU KNOW?

Marsupial frogs care for their young in different ways than other frogs. In fact, marsupial frogs act more like mother kangaroos than frogs! Marsupial frogs live in trees. They carry their young on their backs or hips in pockets of skin. In some species, the mother carries her eggs until they hatch into tadpoles. In other species, the male loads little tadpoles into his hip pockets. He carries them until they change into frogs.

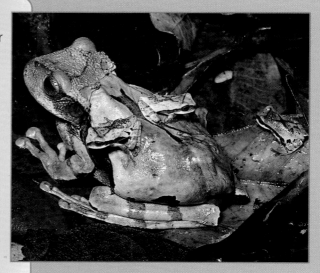

STAYING CLOSE

Male and female common frogs do not care for their babies, but they often stay around the pond where they have laid their eggs.

BABY FILE

1. The adult female frog lays her eggs in the water.

2. The tadpole hatches from its egg. It starts to swim, breathing through gills.

3. Back legs and then front legs grow on the little tadpole. When it develops lungs, it begins to gulp air at the surface of the water.

4. The tail becomes smaller and slowly disappears. The young frog leaves the water and hops on land.

BIRTH

The mother common frog lays up to four thousand black eggs. A protective coating that looks like jelly covers each egg. From ten to twenty-one days later, the eggs hatch into tadpoles. First, the tadpoles eat their jelly coats. Later, they eat tiny green water plants. Soon, the tadpoles grow feathery gills.

SIX TO NINE WEEKS

In about six to nine weeks, the tadpoles grow legs. They also develop lungs and swim to the surface of the water to breathe air. These tiny tadpoles are big eaters. They munch on plants and insects.

THREE MONTHS TO THREE YEARS

When the frogs are three to four months old, they lose their tails. They jump out of the water and start their lives on land. Young frogs continue to grow for two or three more years. They are full grown by the age of three. Then they lay eggs and start families of their own.

A Noisy Life

Sounds are very important to frogs, and each kind of frog has its own song. Male frogs sing to attract females and to warn rival frogs to stay away. A frog makes its sounds by forcing air out of its lungs and across its **vocal cords**. In some frog species, the male has a vocal sac that swells like a balloon when he makes sounds. A vocal sac helps make a frog's song louder. Some female frogs can make sounds, but they are much quieter than males!

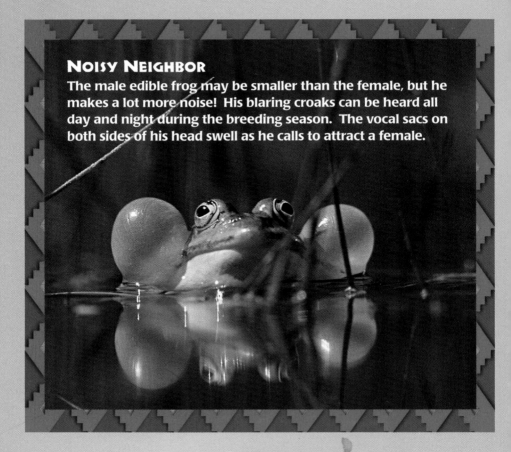

Noisy Neighbor
The male edible frog may be smaller than the female, but he makes a lot more noise! His blaring croaks can be heard all day and night during the breeding season. The vocal sacs on both sides of his head swell as he calls to attract a female.

Big Bubble

The male painted reed frog might be tiny, but he can whistle loudly. When he sings, the vocal sac on his chin fills with air. The vocal sac can be bigger than his body!

Spring Peeper

A small frog called a spring peeper lives in the eastern part of North America. Its name comes from its call, which sounds like bells in springtime. The frog fills a vocal sac under its chin with air to make a louder call. Its call can be heard from 1 mile (1.6 kilometers) or more away!

Favorite Foods

Frogs are predators, which means that they eat other animals. Unlike some predators, frogs usually do not chase their prey. Instead, frogs wait quietly for their prey to get close. Many kinds of frogs have colors and patterns that help **camouflage** them. When a frog spots a meal, it flicks out its tongue. The sticky tip of its tongue can catch the prey and hold it so it cannot get away. The frog curls its tongue back into its mouth, swallowing its prey alive.

Finding a Frog

Frogs are not fast enough to catch food or great at fighting enemies. Instead, frogs try to hide from prey and predators. A common frog can change the color of its skin to look like the plants in its **habitat**.

- Tadpoles feed mainly on tiny water plants, but they sometimes attack small water bugs, too.

- Most frogs have small teeth on their top jaws. They do not have teeth on their bottom jaws, so they usually swallow their food whole.

- Some kinds of frogs are prepared if they eat something poisonous. A frog of this type can throw up its entire stomach! The frog wipes its stomach clean with its legs.

- A group of frogs is called an army. A group of toads is called a knot.

WIGGLY MOUTHFUL

An earthworm spends most of its life beneath the ground. It digs its way through the earth, eating the soil. If the weather is wet, worms crawl up to the surface, and frogs feast on the wiggly meal.

MEATY MEAL

Slugs may not look like a tasty meal to you, but frogs love them. A frog sits very still, waiting for a slug to slither past. When a slug moves into the frog's range, the frog snaps out its tongue. It can catch the surprised slug in an instant.

DANGER!

The world is a dangerous place for frogs. At all stages of its life — egg, tadpole, and adult — a frog faces enemies on land and in water. Badgers, otters, hedgehogs, snakes, raccoons, bats, and owls hunt young and adult frogs alike on land. In water, fish, ducks, newts, and insects wait to feast on frogs, tadpoles, and even eggs. Another danger for frog eggs is dry weather. Most species of frog eggs do not hatch if they do not stay moist.

WELCOME FEAST

The gray heron waits, standing knee-deep in water, for a fish or a frog to swim by. Suddenly, it strikes! It stabs downward with its long, pointed bill to snatch its victim. With a toss of its beak, it swallows its prey whole.

SLEEK SWIMMER

An otter is not a fussy feeder. It needs a lot of food to survive, and it eats any prey it can catch — even frogs! Frogs are not helpless, though. Some frogs scream when they are caught, scaring the predator so much that it lets go of its victim. Other frogs have poison in their skin that burns the predator's mouth until it drops its catch.

TRAPPED!

The young, or larvae, of the dragonfly live in freshwater. Dragonfly larvae are known as fierce predators, and they are sometimes called water tigers. The larvae use their special hooked jaws to grab and trap little animals, such as tadpoles, growing up in a pond or river.

PRICKLY HUNTER

Hedgehogs come out at night to hunt, snuffling through the grass and sniffing out dinner. The foods they eat most are insects and **arachnids**, but a frog can make a good dinner for a hedgehog, too.

23

A Frog's Day

6:00 AM

It was almost dawn. I gave a few loud croaks to tell all the other frogs that I am the biggest and best frog here!

7:00 AM

I started the day with a swim, diving down to the bottom of the pond and back up to the top again. It was nearly time for breakfast!

8:00 AM

Hunting for my meal didn't take long. I sat very still on some leaves near the pond. A big beetle crawled past. I flicked my tongue – breakfast!

10:00 AM

I left the pond for a while and stretched my legs by leaping through the long grass. Then I rested in the moist ground under some stones.

12:00 NOON

It was a warm day, and I decided to go back to the water for another swim. At the pond, I saw some of my cousins. We don't live together, but we do bump into each other now and then.

4:00 PM

It would soon be dark. I hid in the leaves, waiting for prey to pass by. In no time, I caught a huge, slimy slug for a snack.

6:00 PM The moon peeked out. I joined the chorus of frogs. We all croaked our noisy greeting. I waited for a female to answer my call.

10:00 PM A female arrived and laid her eggs in the water. The new frog spawn glistened in the moonlight. Soon, lots of little tadpoles will swim in our pond!

12:00 MIDNIGHT I saw a cat hiding in the undergrowth, so I croaked loudly to warn the others. Then I jumped into the water. Cats eat frogs — if they can catch us!

2:00 AM I was hungry for another snack, so I hopped over to the nearby bushes. I reached out and grabbed a big moth as it fluttered past me.

5:00 AM The sky is growing light. A fish came up to the surface of the pond, and with one gulp, it swallowed a huge mouthful of tiny tadpoles. We lose a lot of our young to predators.

RELATIVES

Frogs and toads belong to the same big group of animals. They have many features in common, but it is easy to see the differences between frogs and toads. Toads have fatter bodies, shorter legs, and drier skin than most frogs. Toads have bumps on their bodies. On land, toads waddle and crawl, while frogs hop and jump.

The midwife toad does not lay its eggs in water like a frog. The father wraps the eggs around his back legs and carries them with him. To keep the eggs wet, the male midwife toad dips all the eggs into water. When the eggs hatch, the father takes the tadpoles to the pond and lets them go.

TOP TOAD

The cane toad, which lives in South and Central America, is the biggest toad in the world. This toad grows to be about the size of a small cat. If a small animal tries to eat a cane toad, the results can be deadly. A cane toad makes enough poison to kill a dog!

FROG FEATS

Types of frogs known as tree frogs have special toes. On the bottom of each flat, wide toe is a pad. These pads act like suckers, gripping the smoothest bark or leaf. Tree frogs can even walk up windows!

The European green tree frog spends most of its life in trees. To stay hidden in its leafy home, it can change color. In the sunshine, this small frog looks bright green. When the weather turns cloudy, the green tree frog changes to a dull gray, which helps it hide in the shadows.

HUMANS AND FROGS

Frogs and toads fascinate some people but frighten others. Some people travel around the world to study how certain kinds of frogs or toads live and behave. Other people are afraid to touch the skin of any kind of amphibian. People keep some kinds of frogs as pets and eat other kinds! In many parts of the world, people have spoiled the natural habitats of frogs and toads. Now, more and more types of frogs and toads are becoming rare.

FEARSOME FROGS

Many kinds of frogs make poisons in their skin. Most frogs do not make enough poison to do more than irritate the skin of a predator, but the poison of a few kinds of frogs can hurt or even kill a human! A poison arrow frog is one of the deadliest animals in the world. Its bright colors warn people and predators to stay away.

FLYING FROG

A frog from the rain forests of Asia doesn't just hop. The flying frog glides between trees using its huge feet. It leaps into the air and stretches out the webbed skin between its toes. The skin works like little parachutes as the frog glides up to 40 feet (12 meters) at a time. As people destroy rain forests, flying frogs are losing their habitat.

African sharp-nosed frogs are very jumpy. This little hopper is only about 2 inches (5 centimeters) long, or about as long as a child's thumb. An African sharp-nosed frog can jump more than 16 feet (5 m) at one time. That long leap would be about the same as an adult man jumping nearly 500 feet (150 m)!

GIANT FROG

The largest frog is the African giant, or Goliath, frog. This king-sized frog grows up to 1 foot (30 cm) long and weighs as much as a pet cat. It is thirty times bigger than its relative, the Cuban frog.

Glossary

ARACHNIDS
A big group of animals, including spiders and scorpions, that mainly live on land, have four pairs of legs, and do not have backbones or antennae.

BREED
To come together for the purpose of producing young.

BURROW
To dig a tunnel or hole in the ground.

CAMOUFLAGE
To hide by using a color, pattern, or appearance that blends in with the surroundings.

GILLS
The organs on the sides of fish through which they breathe.

HABITAT
The natural setting in which plants and animals live.

HIBERNATE
To spend a long period of cold weather in a kind of deep sleep during which all body functions slow down.

MAMMALS
Warm-blooded animals that have backbones and hair or fur on their skin and that feed their young with milk from the mother.

MATES
Animals that partner with other animals to create or raise young.

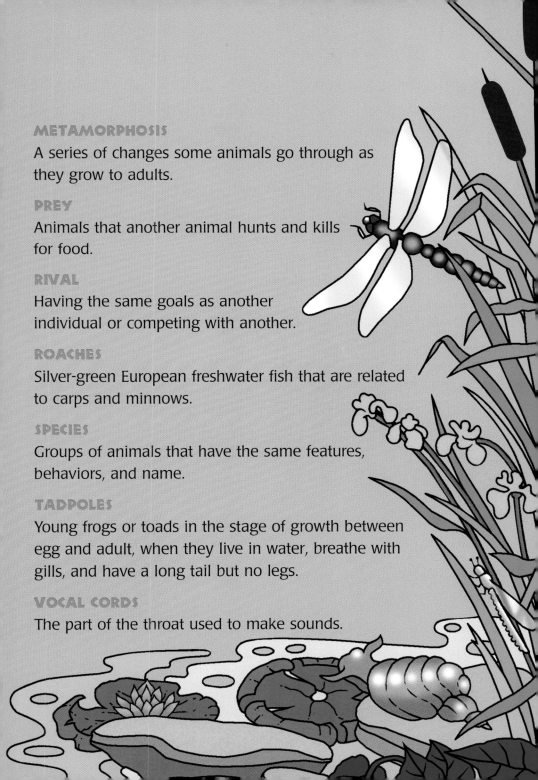

METAMORPHOSIS
A series of changes some animals go through as they grow to adults.

PREY
Animals that another animal hunts and kills for food.

RIVAL
Having the same goals as another individual or competing with another.

ROACHES
Silver-green European freshwater fish that are related to carps and minnows.

SPECIES
Groups of animals that have the same features, behaviors, and name.

TADPOLES
Young frogs or toads in the stage of growth between egg and adult, when they live in water, breathe with gills, and have a long tail but no legs.

VOCAL CORDS
The part of the throat used to make sounds.

Index